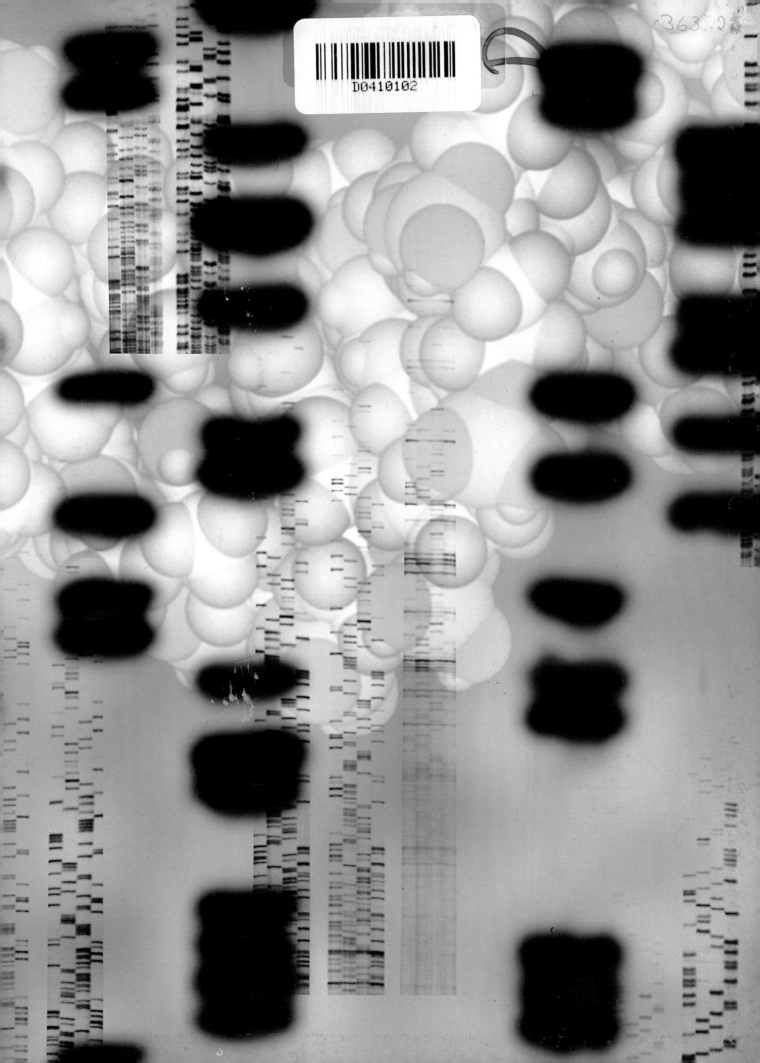

CRIMINAL INVESTIGATION

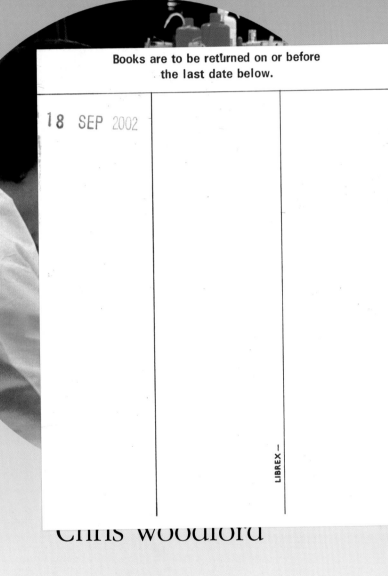

Chris Woodford

an imprint of Hodder Children's Books

SCIENCE FACT FILES

CRIMINAL INVESTIGATION · COMMUNICATIONS
THE EARTH'S RESOURCES · ELECTRICITY AND MAGNETISM
FORCES AND MOTION · GENETICS
THE HUMAN BODY · LIGHT AND SOUND
THE SOLAR SYSTEM · WEATHER

Produced by Roger Coote Publishing
Gissing's Farm, Fressingfield
Suffolk IP21 5SH

First published in 2001 by Hodder Wayland
An imprint of Hodder Children's Books
Text copyright © 2001 Hodder Wayland
Volume copyright © 2001 Hodder Wayland

Design and typesetting Victoria Webb
Commissioning Editor Lisa Edwards
Editors Alex Edmonds and Jon Ingoldby
Picture Researcher Lynda Lines
Illustrator Alex Pang

Endpaper picture: DNA fingerprint and part of a DNA molecule
Title page picture: An FBI forensic scientist examining a handgun

We are grateful to the following for permission to reproduce photographs: Associated Press 40 (Pablo Martinez Monsivais); Camera Press 26 (Ray Hamilton), 28 left (L Schiller), 35 (Gavin Smith), 42, 43 bottom (Kathy Amerman); Corbis 9 bottom (AFP), 14 bottom (Paul Velasco/Gallo Images), 15 top (Joseph Sohm/Chromo Sohm Inc), 31 (Jim Sugar), 39 (Richard T Nowitz), 41 top (Reuters MewMedia Inc); Oxford Scientific Films 30 top (RL Manuel), 30 bottom (Alastair Macewan), 32 top (David Cayless), 32 bottom (RL Manuel); Rex Features 11 bottom (J Sutton Hibbert), 12 top (Fiona Jones), 15 bottom, 19 top (SIPA), 27 left (Nils Jorgensen), 34 top and bottom (SIPA), 43 top (SIPA/Ira Strickstein); Science and Society Picture Library/Science Museum 33 bottom; Science Photo Library front cover main image (Alfred Pasieka), front cover top (Dr Jurgen Scriba), front endpaper (Alfred Pasieka), 5 (Peter Menzel), 8 (Peter Menzel), 10 (Pascal Goetcheluck), 12 bottom (Peter Menzel), 16 (Manfred Kage), 17 top (Philippe Plailly), 17 bottom (Philippe Plailly), 18 (Peter Menzel), 19 bottom (Dr Jurgen Scriba), 21 (Biophoto Associates), 23 top (Michel Viard/Peter Arnold Inc), 24 (Tek Image), 25 bottom (Geoff Tompkinson), 27 right (Adam Hart-Davis), 41 bottom (Peter Menzel); Shout Pictures 9 top, 36, 37 top, 38; Stock Market front cover bottom (Al Francekevich), 22 (Al Francekevich); Stone 20 (Julie Houck), 33 top (Roger Tully); Topham Picturepoint 13 top (David Giles), 23 bottom, 28–9, 29 bottom, 37 bottom (Stephan Rousseau).

The statistics given in this book are the most up to date available at
the time of going to press.

Printed in Hong Kong by Wing King Tong

A CIP catalogue record for this book is available from the British Library

ISBN 0 7502 3184 X

Hodder Children's Books
A division of Hodder Headline Limited
338 Euston Road, London NW1 3BH

CONTENTS

The words that are explained in the glossary are printed in **bold** the first time they are mentioned in the text.

INTRODUCTION

Solving a crime is rather like piecing together a jigsaw puzzle. Police officers may arrive at the scene of a crime within minutes, but it usually takes weeks, months or even years to collect enough **evidence** to find out why a crime was committed and who committed it. Despite many years of painstaking effort, some crimes are never solved.

Detectives

Investigating crimes is the job of police officers known as detectives. They are responsible for finding out who has committed crimes and for bringing these people to justice. In the UK, detectives work for a branch of the police called the Criminal Investigation Department or CID. In the USA, detectives may work for a state or city police department or for a national criminal investigation agency, such as the Federal Bureau of Investigation (FBI).

The same detectives normally follow a case all the way from when it is first discovered to when a **suspect** is tried for the crime in court. They examine the crime scene, piece together the evidence (clues from the scene), find likely suspects (people who might have committed the crime) and try to link one or more of these suspects to the crime.

Detectives carefully photograph the scene of a crime. Every piece of evidence must be recorded, no matter how small, before the scene is disturbed or any articles are removed from it.

EARLY FORENSIC SCIENCE

Forensic science is much older than most people believe. Fingerprint patterns have been detected on ancient cave paintings and the Chinese were using them to identify people as long ago as 700 CE (Common Era).

Many important advances were made in the nineteenth century. Toxicology (the study of poisons) was pioneered in 1813 by a Spanish chemist called Matthieu Orfila (1787–1853). **Anthropometry** (a way of identifying people by measuring parts of the body) was developed by a French policeman, Alphonse Bertillon (1853–1914), in 1883. The modern system of fingerprinting dates from 1896.

Forensic laboratories are a more recent development. The first laboratory in the USA was set up in California in 1923. The FBI set up its own technical laboratory in Washington, D.C. in 1932 and, three years later, a similar laboratory was set up by Scotland Yard, the detective branch of London's Metropolitan Police.

Forensic scientists use a range of special tools.

Forensic science is a good example of how science can be used in everyday life. Without the help of forensic scientists, many crimes would go unsolved and many criminals would never be caught.

Traces of explosives found on Timothy McVeigh's clothing helped the FBI to link him to a bombing in Oklahoma City in 1995 that killed 168 people and injured 500 more.

Forensic science

Detectives do not work alone. Usually, they are helped by a number of specially trained police scientists and doctors, who try to discover vital pieces of evidence that can solve the crime. Using science and medicine to solve crimes is known as **forensics** or forensic science. It includes everything from examining bloodstains found at the crime scene to studying a person's body to find out why they died. Forensic scientists work directly at the crime scene. They also take away evidence from the scene and examine it more carefully in a police laboratory.

French forensic scientists investigate a body found in a forest.

Crimes can happen anywhere: inside someone's house, at a bus stop, or even in the middle of the street. A criminal investigation always starts at the crime scene. This is not just the area where the crime has taken place – it's also where police officers are most likely to find the evidence they will need to solve it.

Detectives are not always the first people to arrive at the crime scene. Often, a uniformed police officer arrives first, perhaps in response to an emergency call. Whoever gets there first, the important thing is always to prevent the crime scene from being disturbed. This is known as 'containing the scene'.

Containing the scene

Suppose someone has been murdered inside his or her home. The killer may have left footprints or fingerprints, dropped an item of clothing or left spots of blood behind. If other people arrive at the scene afterwards, they too may leave footprints, fingerprints and other marks. These may confuse the scientists who are analyzing the scene. Worse, if people take away evidence from the scene, detectives who investigate later may be unable to find the vital clues they need to solve the crime and catch the killer.

Containing the scene means keeping all the evidence in place until it has been properly recorded and collected. This might involve closing a building to the public or sealing off an area outside with special tape marked 'POLICE LINE: DO NOT CROSS'.

Recording the scene

Crime scenes cannot be contained forever, especially if they are outside in public places. For this reason, detectives usually make notes about what they can see and draw sketches of the scene. They may also take large numbers of photographs or make video recordings. Records of a crime scene must be precise enough to be able to recreate the scene later, if necessary.

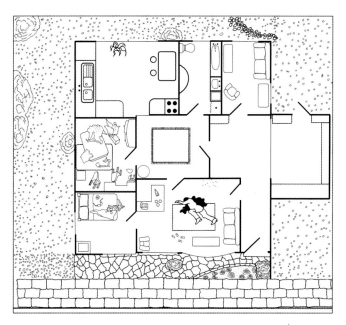

A crime scene sketch shows the location of the murder victim and other key pieces of evidence.

FACT FILE

THE BOMB SCENE

One of the biggest dangers to police officers comes from crime scenes where explosives have been used. According to the FBI, there were over 38,000 such incidents in the United States alone between 1988 and 1997. Around two thirds of these attacks were directed at people's homes, vehicles and mailboxes.

When detectives arrive at a bomb scene, the first thing they need to be sure about is that the scene is safe for them to enter. In April 1999, 15 people were killed when two former school students ran amok with firearms and explosives at Columbine High School in Colorado. Even after the shootings had finished, it took many hours for bomb squad officers to declare the scene safe. After two very thorough searches with bomb-detecting robots and specially trained dogs, more than 30 explosive devices and a car bomb had been recovered from the school campus. Only then did officers finally realize the extent of the terrible tragedy that shocked people around the world.

They must also be carefully prepared so they can be used as evidence in court. Although sketches of the scene may be rough, they are usually marked with precise measurements to show exactly where evidence was first found. Police photographs often include pictures of rulers to give an idea of the scale of the objects being shown. Sketches and photographs are usually taken from many different angles to provide a complete record of the scene.

Forensic scientists record fingerprints at a crime scene.

COLLECTING EVIDENCE

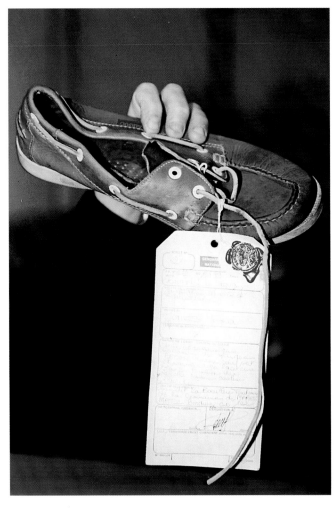

Once the crime scene has been recorded, evidence can be collected together, ready to be taken away for examination in the police laboratory. Evidence is collected either by detectives themselves or by forensic scientists (sometimes known as 'scene of crime' officers). Any evidence must be carefully stored and protected against tampering, from the time it is collected to the time it is presented in court. This is known as maintaining the **chain of evidence**.

This shoe was an important piece of evidence in a French murder case.

A blood sample is taken from a shirt found at a crime scene.

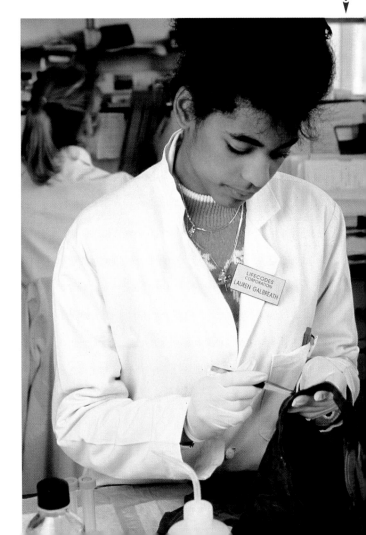

 **FACT FILE**

IN THE JEANS
Criminals often go to great lengths not to leave evidence at the crime scene, but they can still be caught in some unexpected ways. Detectives from the FBI recently managed to identify a bank robber from a security video showing only his jeans. The blue denim had worn in such a unique pattern that it identified the robber almost as well as a fingerprint!

Evidence is collected from a car abandoned at a crime scene. Special 'POLICE' tape was used to seal off the crime scene until the forensic scientist arrived.

Types of evidence

Evidence may tell a detective what crime has been committed, how it was committed and who committed it. For example, broken glass inside a window may show where thieves entered a house to carry out a burglary, while broken glass outside may show where they left. The most important evidence helps to prove that a certain person was at the crime scene and could have carried out the crime. Fingerprints, bloodstains, hairs from suspects, traces of fibres or threads, marks made by tools used to enter or leave a building and traces left by firearms may all help to place a certain suspect at the scene of the crime.

Following the trail

Crime scenes may contain large amounts of evidence. To make sense of it all properly, detectives may try to follow the 'trail' of the crime from its beginning to its end, collecting up evidence as they go. Different types of evidence are gathered and stored in different ways. Pools of blood, for example, may be mopped up on cotton cloth, allowed to dry and refrigerated. This is because biological evidence is best stored dried and cold.

Special techniques

Forensic scientists use many ingenious methods for gathering evidence. Tyre-marks found at a crime scene may be preserved by making a cast. Plaster of Paris, a thick liquid rather like milk shake, is poured into the tyre-mark. It quickly sets into a hard white cast showing the pattern of the tyre-mark in reverse that can be pulled out in one piece. Shoeprints can be recovered in similar ways using either plaster of Paris or special rubber 'shoeprint lifters' which are rather like very thick sticky tape.

Because evidence is not always visible to the naked eye, forensic scientists often examine a crime scene with ultraviolet light (a type of short-wavelength blue light that our eyes cannot see). This shows up body fluids (such as the sweat on fingerprints) by making them fluoresce (glow rather like the way a luminous watch glows in the dark). Samples can then be taken for laboratory analysis.

Police use this remote-controlled robot to investigate bombs.

WITNESSES

Some of the most important evidence in solving a crime may not come directly from the crime scene itself. People nearby who happened to see, hear or notice unusual things when the crime was committed can also provide important clues. Witnesses, as these people are known, may have seen suspicious-looking cars driving by. They may have heard shouts or gunshots. They may even have walked past the criminal in the street. The police need to interview witnesses to find out what they know. The information a witness gives is known as a witness **statement**.

Finding witnesses

When a crime has been committed, police officers try to find as many witnesses as they can. They may work their way systematically around the neighbourhood in what is known as a 'door-to-door inquiry' asking people whether they saw or heard anything. They may set up roadblocks near the crime scene and interview people driving past. Sometimes, if they cannot find witnesses, they may appeal on local or national television and radio for people to come forward. Just as scientists keep making measurements and taking observations to test their theories, so police officers interview as many witnesses as they can to help build up a clear picture of the crime.

Police question a motorist at a roadblock near a crime scene in South Africa.

FACT FILE

WITNESSES AND EVIDENCE
Criminal investigation sometimes involves interviewing hundreds or thousands of witnesses and trying to make sense of a tremendous amount of evidence. After the tragic shootings at Columbine High School in Colorado on 20th April 1999, detectives interviewed hundreds of children, staff and others in an attempt to understand what had happened. They collected over 10,000 pieces of evidence, took more than 10,000 photographs, inspected over 300 bullet holes and examined over 1,000 pupils' rucksacks abandoned at the scene.

One week later, when British TV crime programme presenter Jill Dando was shot dead outside her London home, Scotland Yard launched one of its biggest ever murder inquiries. A team of 45 detectives interviewed 3,000 people, took 1,000 statements and trawled through 4,000 messages sent to the police incident room. After drawing up a list of 400 suspects, police finally charged a man with the crime a little over a year later.

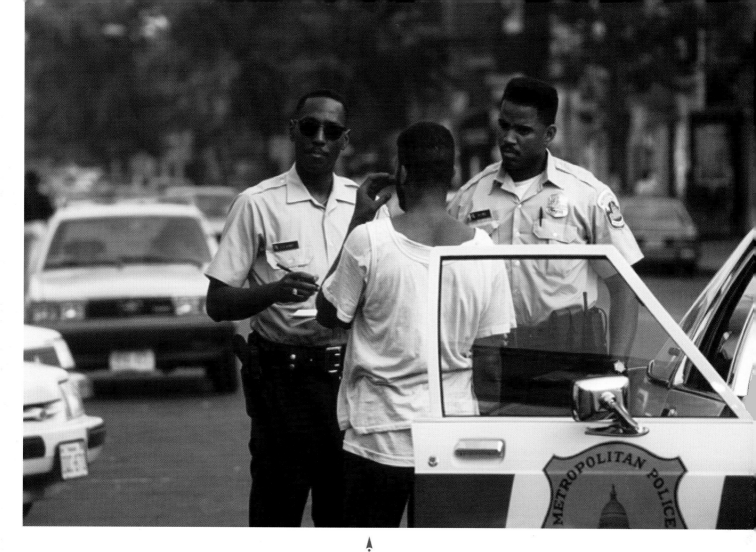

Problems with witness evidence

Witnesses are a vital part of any criminal investigation, but their evidence can still present problems. If some time has passed between the crime and the police inquiry, witnesses may forget important details. Detectives sometimes try to jog the memory of witnesses by reconstructing a crime. For example, if a person has disappeared, a police officer may dress up to look like the missing person and follow his or her last known movements. This is known as a crime **reconstruction**. It may be filmed and shown on television.

Another problem is that different witnesses may see different things or say things that disagree with one another. Psychologists (scientists who study the human mind and the way people behave) have found the questions police ask can affect how witnesses remember an accident or a crime. For example, if a detective trying to find out about a minor car accident asks: 'How did the cars smash into one another?', witnesses will describe a more violent crash than if the detective asks: 'How did the cars collide?'.

Police officers interview a witness in Washington D.C., in the USA. Witnesses are sometimes asked to go to a police station to make a statement.

Detectives in the UK carry out a door-to-door inquiry.

15

FINGERPRINTS

Touch a clean, empty glass with your fingers and hold it up to the light. You will notice patterns of swirling lines that your fingers leave behind. They are known as fingerprints, and are caused by sweat 'printed' onto the surface of the glass by the tiny hills and valleys on your skin. No two people have the same fingerprints. This means detectives can find out whether someone was at the scene of a crime by comparing his or her fingerprints with ones they find at the scene.

Fingerprints at the scene

Fingerprints may be either 'visible' or 'latent'. As the name suggests, visible prints show up by themselves.

Your fingerprints should stay the same throughout your life. They change only because of accidents, illnesses or surgery.

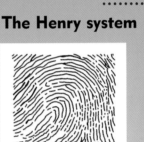

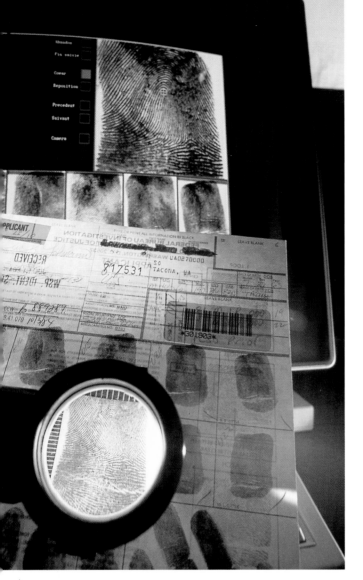

Matching the prints

If fingerprints are found at a crime scene, the next step is to find out who they belong to. If someone has been killed at the scene, do the prints belong to that person? If a burglary has been committed, do the prints belong to the owners of the house or to the criminals?

Whenever people are arrested for crimes, fingerprints are taken by inking their fingers and pressing them onto a card. In this way, police forces around the world have built up large collections of fingerprint records. Once, fingerprints found at a crime scene would have been painstakingly compared with these records to try to find a match. Today, computers can rapidly tell whether prints found at a crime scene match those of a known criminal. Two fingerprints are said to match when 16 specific features of one print match the same features of the other.

Computers help detectives to identify fingerprints quickly and accurately.

A person's fingerprints are scanned into a computer.

They are usually made by criminals whose hands are covered in dirt, soot, blood or ink. Visible prints are easy to spot and can be photographed with little difficulty.

Latent is another word for hidden. Latent prints are the invisible fingerprints produced by perspiration. Before they can be photographed, they have to be made visible in some way. To do this, forensic scientists may brush a powder onto things like tables, windows and light switches at the crime scene to make any latent prints show up. The prints are then lifted off the surface using special tape, and photographed. Latent prints left on materials such as paper and cloth can be made visible with a chemical dye. They are then photographed in the same way.

THE POLICE LABORATORY

Although a great deal of forensic work is done at the crime scene, not everything can be done there. Items that could prove useful as evidence are removed from the scene and taken away to the police laboratory for more detailed examination. There may be several different laboratories in a forensics department, each specializing in a different type of scientific work.

Cutting-edge equipment

Police laboratories are usually equipped with the very latest scientific equipment and staffed by highly trained forensic scientists who may be experts in physics, chemistry, biology and medicine. Microscopes may be used to inspect items from the crime scene more closely. Complex machines known as **spectrometers** are used to identify what sort of chemicals are present in unknown substances that may have been found there. All this equipment is designed for a single purpose: to understand what happened at the scene and to provide information that will help detectives solve the crime.

HISTORY FILE

THE CASE OF WAYNE WILLIAMS

Wayne Williams, one of the most infamous **serial killers** in American history, was found guilty of killing over 20 young men through the fibres that he left on his victims. Some of the fibres were yellow-green, matching an unusual carpet in Williams' home. Different fibres on another victim matched the carpet in Williams' car.

This evidence was very significant, but it was not enough to prove Williams' guilt because the two carpets might have been very common. So FBI detectives set about carefully identifying the carpets in each case and working out how many of each type were likely to be in the part of Georgia where Williams lived. This suggested the chance of Williams accidentally being linked to both types of fibre were almost 30 million to 1. On the strength of this and other evidence, Williams was found guilty of the murders in 1982.

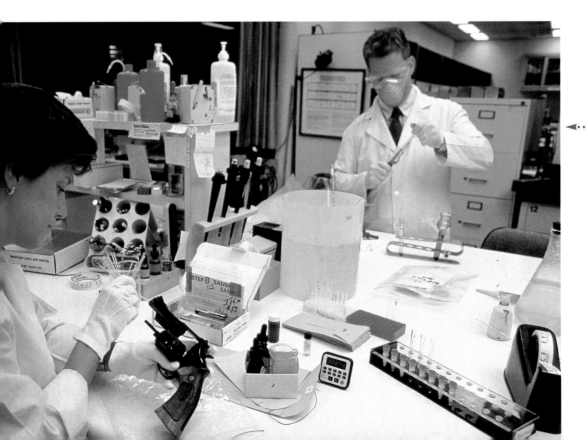

These scientists work at the FBI's laboratory in Washington, D.C. in the USA. They are testing a gun for traces of blood.

Ingenious experiments

Some of the tests carried out in police laboratories are quite ingenious. A piece of simple equipment known as an electrostatic detection apparatus (ESDA) can show up handwriting left behind on documents or books after the top sheets of paper have been removed. First, the sample document is placed over a flat piece of metal, tilted at an angle and covered with thin plastic film (similar to food wrap). This is sucked down tightly by an air pump and a large static electrical charge is passed over it.

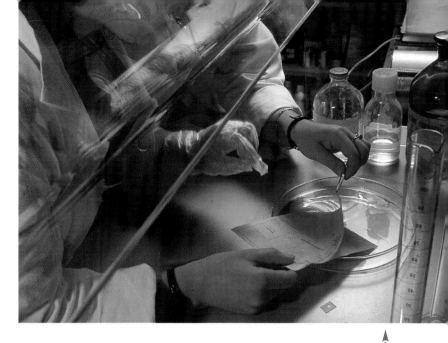

Forensic scientists test a document found at a crime scene. The ink and paper used may give detectives important clues.

FUTURE FILE

THE SIMS GUN

One of the latest pieces of equipment for forensic analysis is called a secondary ion mass spectrometer (SIMS) gun. A minute sample of material from the crime scene is loaded into the apparatus and then blasted with a beam of charged particles (ions) from the gun. Atoms or molecules from the sample are broken free by the beam and collected for analysis. Using the SIMS gun, forensic scientists can now find evidence in even the smallest traces from a crime scene.

Toner (fine powdered ink like that used in photocopiers) is sprinkled over the upright document. Most of it falls straight down the paper and collects at the bottom, but some sticks in the hollows on the paper caused by the handwriting impressions. In a short time, the hidden handwriting magically appears!

This scanning electron microscope (see page 21) can magnify samples from a crime scene by up to 40,000 times.

FORENSIC ANALYSIS

One of the most important jobs for the police laboratory is identifying tiny traces of evidence found at the scene. This might include inks used on documents, dirt from the shoeprints left by a criminal, tiny flakes of nail varnish, or swabs from a suspect's hands that may reveal the powder from a gunshot.

Another important job is comparing samples taken from a suspect with samples from the scene and trying to prove the two are the same. When the evidence from two different places is identical, the forensic scientist has established what is called a **physical match**. This may be enough to convict a criminal in court.

Scientific method

Because it is not always obvious what substances are when they are first discovered, forensic scientists have to test them in various ways. Just like other scientists, they carry out a variety of experiments and carefully observe the results. Depending on what they find, they come up with theories about what a substance might be. Then they carry out more experiments to find out if those theories are correct and to confirm the substance is what they think it is.

FACT FILE

GAS CHROMATOGRAPHY

Gas chromatography helps to reveal what a substance is by breaking it up into the chemicals from which it is made. A sample is injected, with gas, into a long coiled tube packed with very small grains of a solid. The different chemicals in the sample creep at different speeds through the tube and get to the end at different times. This is because each chemical component has a different chemical property that affects its movement through the tube. A sensitive detector attached to the tube measures this and a computer draws a graph of the results. Each line (peak) of the graph shows a different chemical in the sample. The graph is a 'chemical fingerprint', because the pattern of peaks is different for every substance.

This police chemist is using gas chromatography to identify samples taken from a crime scene.

Electron microscope

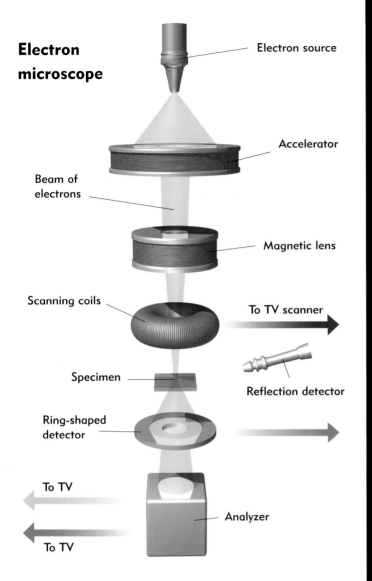

- Electron source
- Accelerator
- Beam of electrons
- Magnetic lens
- Scanning coils
- To TV scanner
- Specimen
- Reflection detector
- Ring-shaped detector
- To TV
- Analyzer
- To TV
- To TV

ELECTRON MICROSCOPE

An ordinary microscope works by bouncing light rays off a sample and using lenses to project a bigger image of the object into our eyes. But there is a limit to the size of things we can see with an ordinary microscope because of the 'size' of light itself: things that are smaller than the wavelength of light cannot be seen.

Instead of using light, an electron microscope bounces a beam of electrons off the object and uses electromagnets instead of lenses and mirrors. Electrons are the tiny particles that spin around inside atoms. They can show up much smaller objects than light rays. In fact, the most powerful electron microscopes can magnify by around 10 million times.

How an electron microscope works

An electron microscope has magnified these human blood cells by 400 times.

This process of carrying out experiments, thinking up theories and testing the theories is called the scientific method.

Identifying a substance

Forensic scientists may begin by looking at a sample (a small amount of the substance) under a microscope. If the sample is too small to show up properly, they might put it under a more powerful electron microscope.

While microscopes can be useful for identifying tiny objects, they don't reveal what those objects are made of. Suppose detectives find a mysterious powder on the carpet at the crime scene. Gas chromatography can help them find out whether they have found some kind of drug, some special kind of sand that might trace the killer or just ordinary household dust.

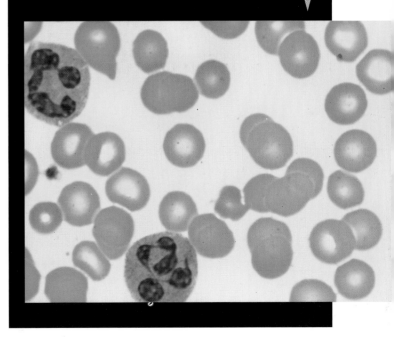

BALLISTICS

Firearms such as handguns and rifles are often involved in violent crimes. The evidence they leave behind can provide important clues for detectives. A bullet found at the scene may help to trace the gun that fired it. The place where the bullet is found may give important information about where the gun was fired from. The study of how bullets are fired and how they travel is called ballistics.

Firearm fingerprints

Guns are designed to spin bullets around as they travel through the barrel, because spinning objects travel much more steadily and accurately. A gun spins its bullets using tiny grooves cut into the inside of the barrel. The barrel also cuts matching grooves into the sides of the bullet as it passes through it at very high speed.

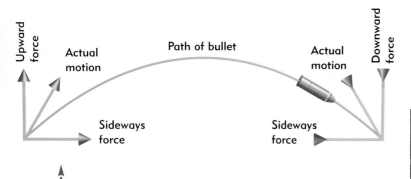

When a bullet is fired upwards, horizontal and vertical forces act on it. These make it follow a curved path called a parabola.

The marks on a bullet can be used to identify it and link it to the gun from which it was fired.

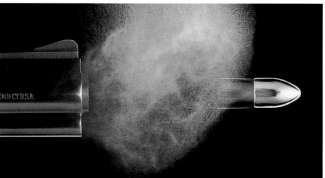

HISTORY FILE

THE ASSASSINATION OF JOHN F. KENNEDY

Probably no crime in history has caused more controversy than the assassination of US President John F. Kennedy ('JFK'). He was shot and killed by a gunman in Dallas, Texas on 22nd November 1963 while riding in an open-top limousine. The gunman was thought to have been a former US marine called Lee Harvey Oswald. He was believed to have fired a single bullet from the sixth floor of the nearby Texas Schoolbook Depository building. But some people believe more than one gunman was involved and that they fired from different places.

Different theories about how JFK might have been killed have been tested by examining the bullet-marks in his body and drawing lines back to where a gun could have been fired from. The path of a bullet is called its trajectory. This type of trajectory analysis has proved that JFK could have been killed by Oswald from the Texas Schoolbook Depository, although the truth of what happened in November 1963 will probably never be known.

This photograph was taken seconds after JFK was shot. The white arrow shows JFK's foot. The black arrow shows other passengers taking cover.

A police marksman tests a gun.

In fact, every gun leaves a distinctive 'fingerprint' of marks called 'lands' and 'grooves' on the bullets it fires. These can be used to match a bullet to the gun that fired it.

Matching the bullet to the gun

Detectives may recover a bullet from the crime scene and a gun from a suspect's home. To prove that the gun was used at the scene, forensic scientists load it with another bullet and fire it into a tank of water. The water rapidly slows the bullet and prevents it from being damaged. The test bullet and the one from the scene are then placed in a comparison microscope. This is a kind of double microscope that allows the lands and grooves of the two bullets to be compared side by side. After this test, the ballistics expert will declare that there is 'identification' (the gun definitely fired the bullet), 'exclusion' (the gun definitely did not fire the bullet) or 'no conclusion' (there is not enough evidence to match the bullet and the gun, perhaps because the original bullet has been damaged too much).

DNA FINGERPRINTING

DNA (deoxyribonucleic acid) is the genetic material inside the cells of your body; a personal 'barcode' that describes who you are. It is DNA that makes you similar to your parents and different from other people. Although your DNA is different from that of everyone else on the planet (unless you have an identical twin), it is the same in every single cell in your body. This means that a sample of DNA taken from a piece of your hair, your blood or some other part of your body can be used to identify you with almost absolute certainty.

The idea that everyone's DNA is unique also forms the basis of one of the newest and most important forensic tests: DNA fingerprinting (sometimes called 'DNA profiling'). A sample of DNA is taken from a suspect (perhaps by plucking out a hair or running a swab around the mouth). Another sample (such as a strand of hair or a spot of blood) is taken from the crime scene. If the DNA from the two matches up, there is good evidence that the suspect may have committed the crime.

Police store DNA fingerprints on computers so suspects can be quickly identified. DNA databases are used in the UK, the USA, Canada, Germany, Norway, Finland, Belgium and Denmark.

HOW A DNA FINGERPRINT IS TAKEN

DNA fingerprints are produced using the following steps:

1 A sample of DNA is taken from the suspect or the scene.

2 The DNA, which consists of long molecules, is cut into smaller pieces by a substance called a 'restriction enzyme'.

3 A jelly-like substance called agarose gel is poured into a special metal tray to which electrodes (electrical contacts) are attached at either end. The DNA fragments are poured on top of the gel and the electricity is turned on.

4 Different-sized DNA fragments travel at different speeds through the gel, attracted by the electrical charge. Eventually, the fragments become separated in order of size. This part of the process is called gel **electrophoresis** (which means separating molecules using a gel substance and electricity).

5 A nylon membrane is now placed on top of the gel, which soaks up the DNA rather like a paper towel soaks up spilled water. The DNA fragments remain in order on the membrane.

6 A radioactive dye called a probe is now added to the DNA on the nylon membrane.

7 A piece of X-ray film is placed over the nylon membrane. Just as photographic film is sensitive to light, so X-ray film is sensitive to radioactivity.

8 Radioactivity is given off by the probe and makes a distinctive pattern of blobs on the X-ray film. When the film is developed, a pattern of light and dark blobs shows up – the DNA fingerprint.

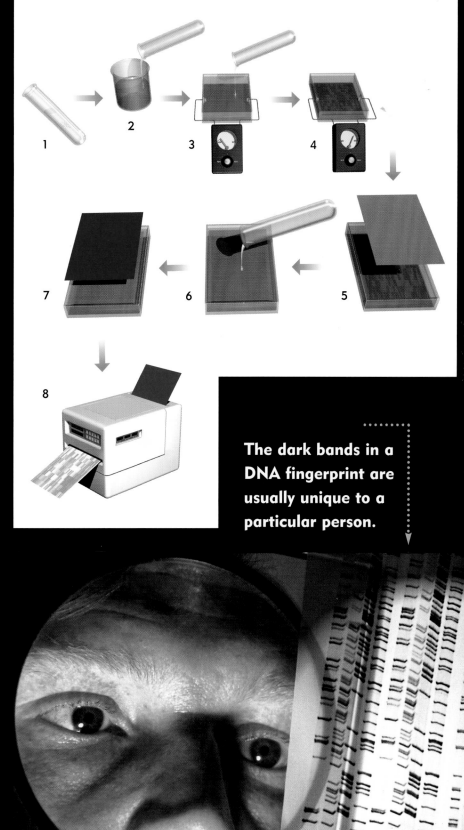

The dark bands in a DNA fingerprint are usually unique to a particular person.

THE CRIMINAL MIND

People commit crimes for a whole variety of reasons. Murders may be committed out of anger or jealousy. Robberies and thefts may happen purely for financial gain. But some crimes are committed because people are mentally ill – because the criminals are 'mad' rather than 'bad'. Serial killers (who kill a series of people, one after another) often fall into this category. It is the job of criminal psychologists (people who try to understand the minds of criminals) to help detectives solve crimes like this. They also help to decide whether a 'criminal' needs punishment or treatment.

FACT FILE

MAD OR BAD?
Murderers are put to death in some countries, but people found to be not guilty because they are insane may be sent to a secure hospital for treatment. So, some criminals try to pretend that they are 'mad' when they are, in fact 'bad'.

In the courtroom, juries must decide whether a person is 'mad' or 'bad'. British courts use the so-called 'McNaughton Rules'. Courts in the USA use a similar test called the 'Brawner Decision'. In simple terms, these rules state that if a person did not know what they were doing when they committed the crime, or did not know that it was wrong, the person is not guilty of the crime because he or she was insane at the time when the crime was committed.

Notorious American killer Charles Manson behaved like a madman in court, but his antics backfired and he was found guilty of seven murders in 1971.

Modus operandi
Serial killers often strike at the same time of day or week, and frequently target a particular type of person. They don't just kill anyone; there is a pattern to their behaviour. Detectives call this pattern a **modus operandi** or MO, which means a plan or way of working. If they can work out a killer's MO, they may be able to predict where the killer will strike next and prevent that crime from taking place. They may also be able to work out the identity of the killer.

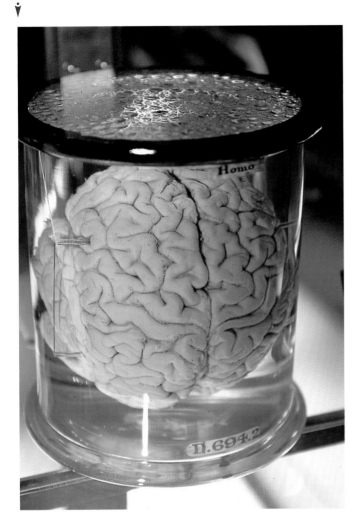

The human brain holds the secrets of a criminal's mind.

Behavioural profiling

Behavioural profiling is a step further into the criminal's mind than working out the MO. It involves a psychologist thinking carefully about the crime that has been committed, the evidence found at the scene and any other clues or information, and trying to work out what sort of a person may have been responsible. The result is a behavioural profile of who the criminal might be. For example, a profile may suggest that a killer is a middle-aged man, living alone, often working away from home and doing an unskilled manual job. A behavioural profile can help to identify likely suspects, but only physical evidence from the crime scene (or a confession from the criminal) can be used to convict them of the crime.

CRIME IN BODY, CRIME IN MIND?
In the nineteenth century, psychologists called 'phrenologists' thought the brain could be divided up like a map of the world, with each region responsible for a different part of our behaviour – for example, 'secretiveness' or 'hope'. Bumps on the head could be used to tell important things about a person's character, including whether they were likely to commit crimes.

In 1895, Italian scientist Cesare Lombroso published a book called *Criminal Anthropology*, in which he explained that murderers had large jaws, but pickpockets had long fingers and beards. Although taken seriously at the time, few people believe these ideas today!

A phrenologist's map of the human brain.

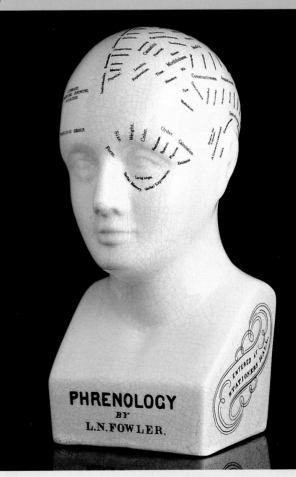

ACCIDENT OR CRIME?

One important use of forensic science is in helping to decide whether people have been killed because of an accident or a crime. Murderers may try to cover their tracks by making a shooting appear as though it were an act of suicide (someone killing themselves). Or men and women may kill their partners and then try to make the crime scene appear as though the killing actually happened during a robbery.

Suicide or murder?

Many different clues can help detectives to tell the difference between an accident and a crime. If a gun is found near a man's dead body, is it close enough to the body for the man to have been able to shoot himself? Are there marks on the man's skin where he pressed the gun to his head?

Actress Marilyn Monroe died of a drug overdose in 1962. But some people believe she was murdered.

Police officers sift through the wreckage of the Lockerbie bomb.

In cases where there is doubt whether a person has shot themselves or been murdered, forensic scientists may do what is called a **gunshot residue** (GSR) test. This involves rubbing cotton swabs moistened with nitric acid over the victim's hands and then examining the swabs for traces of metals, such as barium and antimony, used in gun cartridges. If they are found, the victim probably fired the gun and the death was probably a suicide. If they are not found, the 'suicide' may have been murder.

Famous accidents or famous crimes?

People are killed in accidents every day and their deaths seldom make the news. But deaths are sometimes so shocking and unexpected that people are unable to accept them as accidents. The death of Diana, Princess of Wales in August 1997 is one example of this.

When the Mercedes car carrying the princess lost control at high speed and crashed into a subway tunnel in Paris, suspicion initially fell on a group of nine paparazzi (photographers) who had been chasing her car on motorcycles. Attention also focused on a small white car that was believed to have collided with the princess's limousine just before the accident. But despite a two-year criminal investigation, no evidence of any crime was discovered. The French judge who conducted the investigation ruled that the princess's death was simply a very tragic accident.

The wrecked Mercedes in which Diana, Princess of Wales, was killed.

FORENSIC PATHOLOGY

When someone dies unexpectedly or in strange circumstances, it is important to ensure that a crime has not been committed. This is the job of the forensic **pathologist**. Forensic pathology involves a careful examination of the dead body to find out how, why and when a person died and whether he or she died naturally or through foul play. In the UK, the examination of the body is called a **post-mortem** (a Latin phrase meaning 'after death'). In the USA it is known as an **autopsy** (a Greek word meaning 'see for yourself').

The pathologist as detective

During a post-mortem, a pathologist examines a dead body rather like a forensic scientist examines the wider crime scene, looking for clues, gathering evidence and testing theories. Where a person has suffered multiple injuries, which injury actually killed him or her? How did he or she sustain those injuries? And are the injuries consistent with murder, suicide, an accidental death or a death by wholly natural causes (for example, a heart attack)?

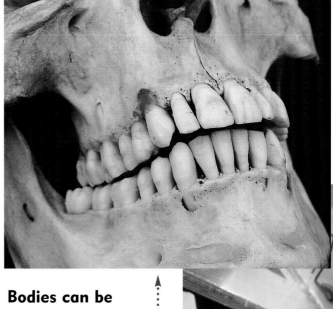

Bodies can be identified from dental records.

FACT FILE

MALE OR FEMALE?
Detectives sometimes discover skeletons, or bodies so badly decomposed, that it is not possible to tell, at first, whether they are men or women. Pathologists can usually help to answer the question by carefully inspecting a skeleton. The size and shape of the skull and the structure of the pelvis area can often be used to work out the sex of a body.

Even a single human hair can provide important clues.

A pathologist dissects (cuts up) a human organ.

The post-mortem

A post-mortem examination usually follows a set procedure. First, the outside of the body is very carefully observed for any marks, such as wounds or bruises. Next, the body is opened and the internal organs (such as the heart, lungs, liver and brain) are removed. Each organ is carefully inspected, weighed and sometimes dissected (cut up into its components). The pathologists keep a record of what they find as they go along, sometimes by speaking into a dictaphone. Samples from the body may be taken to a laboratory for closer examination or analysis. At the end of the post-mortem, the organs are replaced and the body is sewn up. Pathologists always take great care to respect the dignity of the person who died.

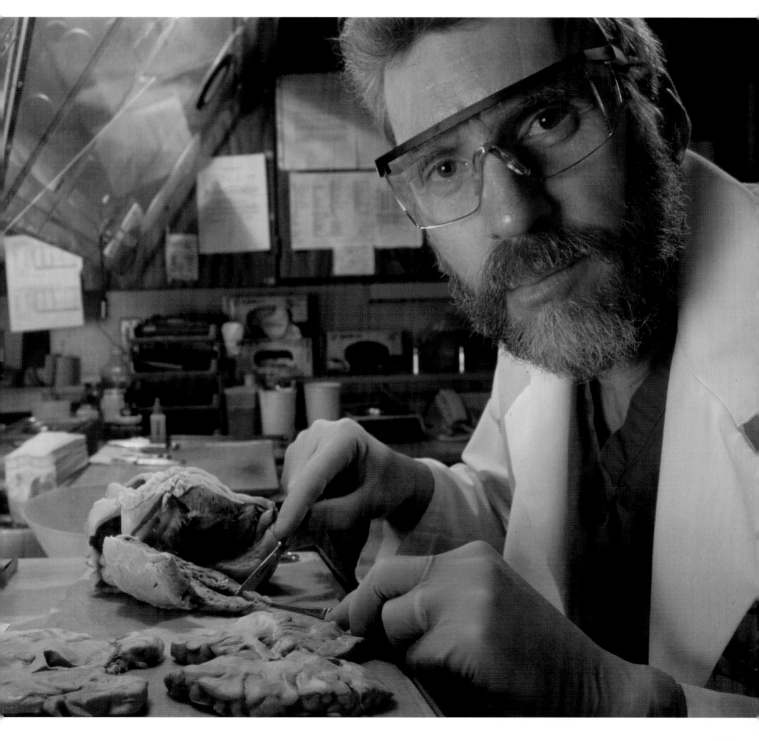

TOXICOLOGY

While pathologists aim to give an account of how and why a person has died, **toxicologists** are called in to explain whether people have died through poisoning. The word 'toxicology' comes from the Greek word *toxicon*, which in ancient times often referred to arrows tipped with poison to increase the likelihood of death.

Types of poisoning

Poisoning does not necessarily mean someone being given a colourful poisonous liquid to drink. In forensic science, it refers to the death or injury caused when too great a dose of a chemical substance has been taken into a person's body. Thus, poisoning can also include an overdose of drink or drugs, breathing in carbon monoxide gas produced during a fire, taking the wrong kind of medicine or accidentally drinking a household chemical. Poisons can be solids (such as the metals cadmium and lead), liquids (such as alcohol) or gases (such as carbon monoxide).

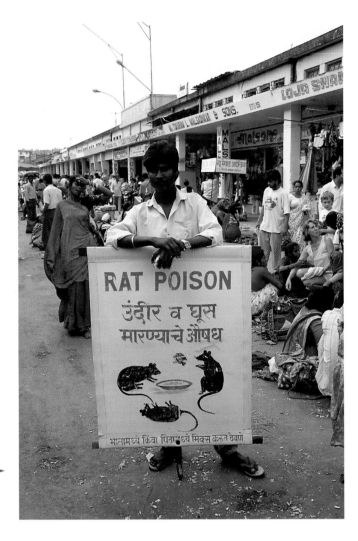

Many household chemicals are poisonous.

Some plants are highly toxic. This deadly nightshade (belladonna) bush contains a toxic chemical called atropine.

Toxicology tests

A toxicologist may carry out a series of experiments on samples taken from a person's body to try to find out how or if poisons were involved in their death. Samples of blood or urine, or tissues cut from the person's internal organs may be tested for drugs, alcohol, known poisons, gases and vapours or other chemicals.

A toxicologist is often involved in cases where detectives are unsure if a death is murder or suicide. Suppose a person's body is recovered from the scene of a fire. Carbon monoxide gas is produced when things burn with too little oxygen present. If the toxicologist finds traces of carbon monoxide in the person's blood, the person must have been alive when the fire started: he or she would have had to breathe in the gas. This could suggest an accidental death. If no carbon monoxide is found, the person was probably dead before the fire started. This suggests murder has taken place and the fire was started to cover it up.

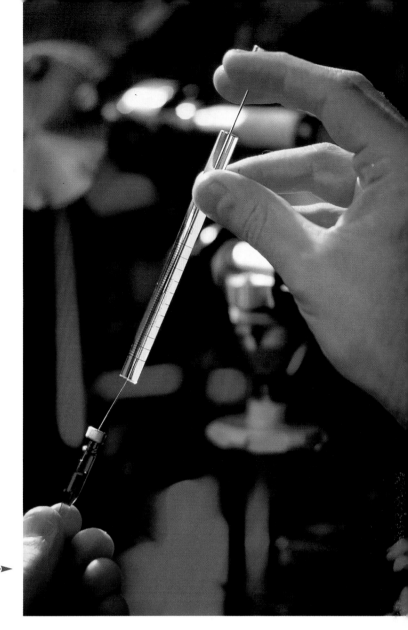

A chemist tries to identify a sample of poison.

 **FACT FILE**

POISONS

Why do poisons kill people? The three main types of poison act in very different ways. Narcotics (notably alcohol and drugs) disrupt important organs or the central nervous system (the body's internal 'telecommunications' network). Corrosives (including acids) burn and destroy the inside of the body. As their name suggests, irritants (such as arsenic) irritate the digestive system, causing pain and vomiting.

Poison bottles from the 19th century.

FORENSIC SCULPTURE

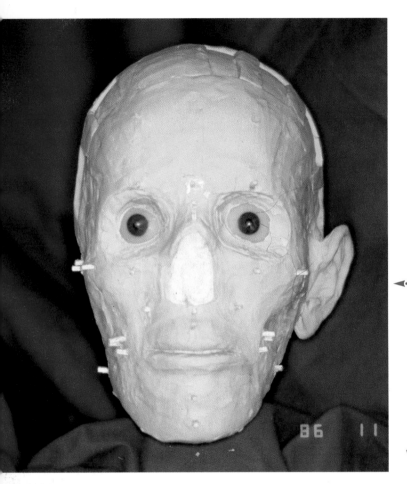

How forensic sculptures are made

One method of forensic sculpture involves building up a clay model of the person's face onto a copy of the skull. Using detailed knowledge of how muscles and tissues are arranged in the human face, the sculptor gradually adds strips of clay to the bare bones. Measurements of the skull size help the sculptor to work out the likely size of the nose and mouth, and where the eyes should be placed. Glass eyes, artificial hair, spectacles and other details may be added later.

The early stages of a clay forensic sculpture. Strips of clay are slowly added and the face is built up layer by layer.

The sculpture is finished off with artificial hair and glass eyes.

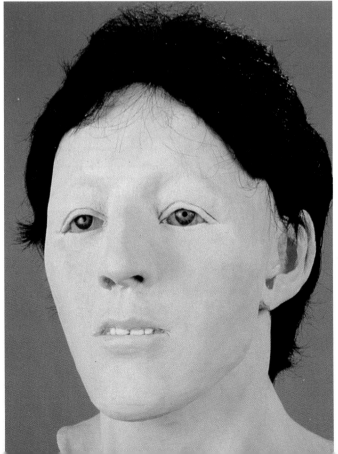

Months or even years may pass between the time when a crime is committed and the time when a body is discovered. After such a long period, the soft tissues of the body decompose and eventually all that remains is the bones of the skeleton. This presents detectives with something of a problem: if all they find is a skeleton, how can they work out who has died or investigate whether a crime has occurred?

Highly trained specialists in human anatomy (the construction of the human body) have developed various methods of making a model of what a person looked like, starting just from the skull. This is called forensic sculpture (or facial reconstruction). Forensic sculptures are often used to trace missing persons. The resemblance between photographs of these people and forensic sculptures produced only from their skulls is often remarkable.

HISTORY FILE

THE HEADLESS BODY RECONSTRUCTION

Forensic sculpture was once used to recreate the face of a man whose head was missing completely. Police found his body in Manchester, England in 1993, but his head was discovered in a shallow pit 80 km away only three months later. The face had been mutilated and the skull had been smashed into 100 pieces to prevent identification. Although almost all the middle of the skull was missing, forensic sculptors managed to piece together the fragments and did their best to reconstruct the man's face. The clay model they made was later successfully identified by a member of the public as a missing Kuwaiti businessman.

Another type of forensic sculpture builds up a computer model of the person instead of a clay model. The skull is placed on a rotating turntable and scanned into the computer using a laser beam. This produces a three-dimensional picture of the skull on the computer screen, to which skin tissues and features can be added. The computer modelling technique is much faster than clay modelling and does not require as much artistic ability and training.

FACT FILE

FACE TO FACE

Reconstructing a human face is a long and difficult process, partly because human anatomy (body structure) is so complex. The skull contains 22 different bones, 14 of them in the face. Around 30 different muscles control our facial expressions. No fewer than 17 of these are needed to make a person smile. All of these muscles are controlled by two major nerves (the communication lines between the parts of our body and our brain). These are the right and left facial nerves, which link directly to the brain.

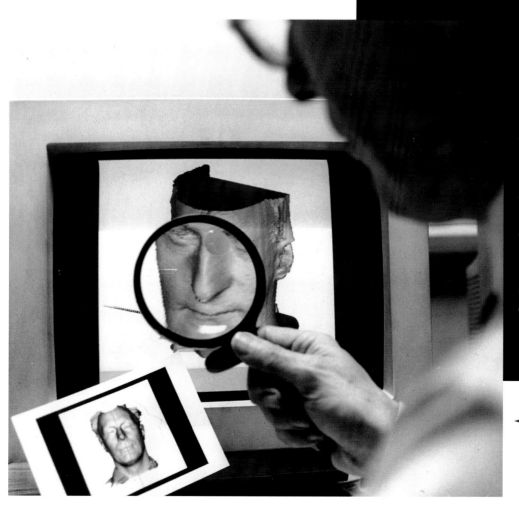

◄ **Reconstructing a face with a computer model.**

35

IDENTIFYING SUSPECTS

Eyewitness evidence is one of the most important ways of finding suspects. If police can get a rough description of what a criminal looks like, it may encourage other witnesses to come forward and it could help to solve the crime.

Remembering the suspect

The human brain is good at recognizing and remembering faces, so police may spend a lot of time helping eyewitnesses to give a good description of what the suspect looks like. There are three main ways of doing this. The simplest method involves a police artist trying to sketch the suspect using a description provided by the witness.

Because witnesses often change their minds as they try to remember details, sketching can take a long time. So, in the 1960s, police throughout the world began to use a quicker system called **Identikit**. Photographs of many different shapes of noses, eyes, mouths, chins, hair and so on, printed onto pieces of plastic, can be put together quickly according to the witness's description to create a 'look-alike' image.

FUTURE FILE

THREE-DIMENSIONAL MUGSHOTS
People tend to look very different from different angles. One problem with police sketches, Identikits and even E-FITs is that they show a suspect only from one angle (usually from the front). A new system being developed at the Massachussetts Institute of Technology (MIT) could soon enable police to produce realistic, three-dimensional sketches of a suspect's face that can be viewed from any direction.

A detective helps a crime victim to make an E-FIT of the person who attacked her.

Today, police forces in 18 different countries use a computerized version of the same idea called E-FIT. Not only can faces be put together more quickly, they can also be aged in various ways and even edited to reflect the way a face decomposes after death.

Today, police forces in 18 different countries use a computerized version of the same idea called E-FIT. Not only can faces be put together more quickly, they can also be aged in various ways and even edited to reflect the way a face decomposes after death.

Finding the suspect

Once police have a good likeness of a suspect, they can use it to appeal for more witnesses, perhaps through newspapers, television or the Internet. When suspects are eventually found, witnesses may be asked to pick them out from a line of innocent people.

Suspects in an identification parade ('lineup').

This is called an identification (ID) parade, or 'lineup'. Because people often don't remember exactly what happened at the time of a crime, ID parades are not always reliable. However, if a suspect is identified by a witness, juries find this evidence very convincing. This has sometimes made ID parades a controversial form of evidence.

Computers can identify suspects automatically from video pictures.

TEST FILE

MAKE YOUR OWN IDENTIKIT
Collect together a large pile of old newspapers and magazines that no one wants any more. Go through them cutting out as many different noses, teeth, eyes, chins and so on as you can find (try to use ones of roughly the same size). Once you've put together a good collection, try to make up faces of famous people, friends or members of your family.

TESTING THE EVIDENCE

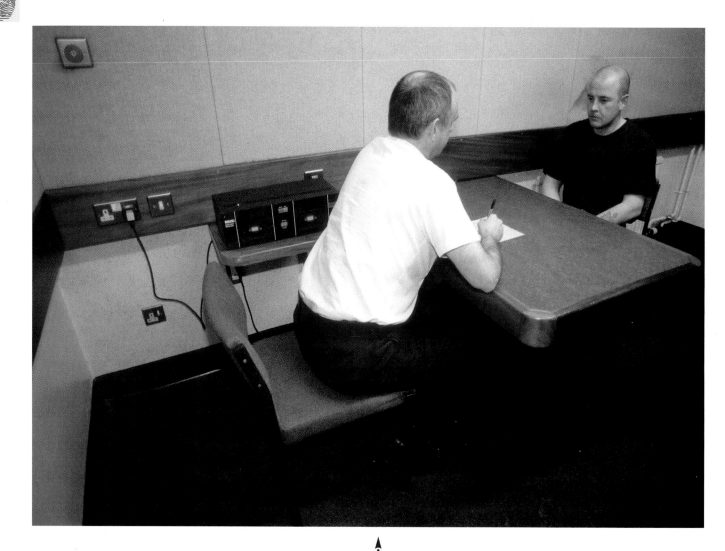

Once police have found their suspect, they may take him or her to the police station for questioning. At this stage of the investigation, detectives may feel confident that they have found the criminal, but they still have to prove a connection between the suspect and the crime.

Linking the suspect to the scene

Forensic tests should, by now, have produced a variety of useful evidence from the crime scene. Detectives may have samples of blood, hair, dirt or fibres. They may have fingerprints or shoeprints. They may have DNA samples. Or they may have found drugs or toxic chemicals. The next step is to find a positive match with the suspect. This might involve taking a fingerprint or DNA sample from the suspect, or getting permission from a court to conduct a thorough search of the suspect's home or workplace.

A police officer interviews a suspect. Their conversation is being tape-recorded for use as evidence.

This is a chance for forensic scientists to find items or substances that match those from the scene.

Interviewing the suspect

While suspects are at the police station, detectives take the opportunity to ask detailed questions about the crime in the hope that a guilty suspect will confess. Until as recently as the 1930s, it was common for the police to employ what are called 'third degree' methods, in which confessions were virtually beaten out of suspects. Today, it is illegal to obtain a confession by force.

FACT FILE

VOICEPRINTS

A voiceprint is a graph showing how the frequency (pitch) of sound produced by someone's voice changes with time. Suppose a kidnapper makes a phone call demanding money and, some months later, detectives arrest a suspect for the crime. They can use a technique called 'voiceprinting' to prove the suspect made the phone call. Scientists believe it is almost impossible for two people to have the same voiceprint, so if the suspect's voiceprint matches that of the kidnapper, detectives have probably solved the crime.

These voiceprints show three different people saying the same words.

Detectives still employ cunning methods to secure a confession, however. These include 'good cop/bad cop', in which one policeman behaves nicely towards the suspect and another behaves horribly. As 'good cop' and 'bad cop' switch back and forth, a guilty criminal is supposed to break down and confess. Another method involves detectives pretending they are the criminal's friends, so the criminal confesses just to unburden her or his mind.

While suspects are being asked questions, they may be wired up to a 'lie detector' (also known as a **polygraph**). This machine produces a graph of various measurements made using electrodes wired up to the suspect's body. A trained operator can usually tell if someone is lying by studying the lie detector graph. However, lie detector evidence is not always reliable and it cannot be used in a court of law.

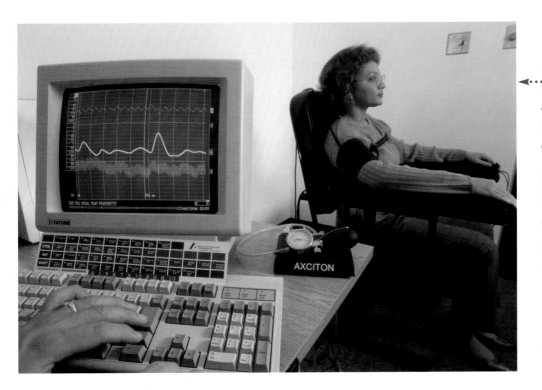

A suspect takes a lie detector test. The peaks in the graph on the screen show whether the suspect is lying or telling the truth.

CRIMINAL RECORDS

Huge amounts of information are collected during a criminal investigation and, with many officers working on a complex case, it can be difficult to make sense of it all. Increasingly, detectives rely on computers to find patterns in evidence and to link the evidence gained from one crime scene to that gained from another. Many countries now have a central computer system that stores general criminal records, and several other specialized systems that are linked to it.

National computers

In the USA, the central information system is the FBI's National Crime Information Computer (NCIC); in the UK, a similar system is called the Police National Computer (PNC). Both systems store details of known criminals, wanted suspects, suspicious vehicles and so on. They can be accessed directly by police officers throughout the country. For example, if a police officer spots a suspicious car near a bank, he or she can radio through to police headquarters to check its registration number. Within seconds, the national computer may come back with information that the vehicle was spotted during a previous bank robbery. The officer at the scene can then take appropriate action.

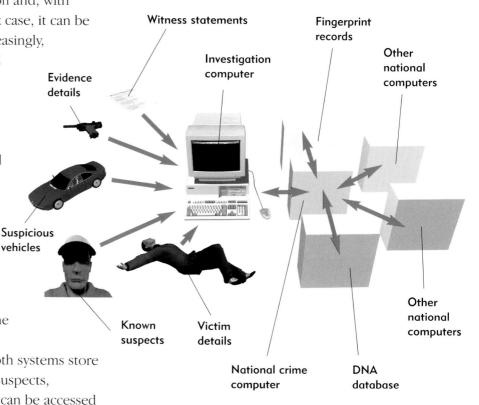

Evidence details

Witness statements

Investigation computer

Fingerprint records

Other national computers

Suspicious vehicles

Known suspects

Victim details

National crime computer

DNA database

Other national computers

Computers record the evidence collected in a major investigation.

The FBI's $20 million operations centre in Washington, D.C., USA.

This Russian forensic scientist is trying to identify soldiers as part of a war crimes investigation.

HISTORY FILE

FINGERPRINT FILES

Fingerprints were among the first criminal records that were systematically kept by detectives. Scotland Yard started its fingerprint collection in 1901 and has several million fingerprints on its computer today. The FBI's collection was started in 1924. Today, it stores something like 250 million sets of prints. If all of the FBI's fingerprint cards were stacked on top of one another, they would make a pile over 130 times higher than the Empire State Building!

Investigation records

Apart from their main computer system, detectives also rely on a number of smaller-scale systems during their investigations. It is increasingly common for all the evidence gathered during a large investigation to be recorded using a computer, so that important clues can be spotted more quickly. In the USA, the FBI has a system called the Investigative Support Information System (ISIS) and at Scotland Yard detectives use a similar computer called HOLMES (Home Office Large Major Enquiry System). Both systems can spot unusual coincidences that may help to identify a suspect. For example, if a certain person was spotted near the scene of two or more related crimes, the computer can highlight him or her as a potential suspect.

Detectives at Scotland Yard in the UK search through fingerprint records.

IN THE COURTROOM

onths or years after a crime has been discovered, a criminal investigation will near its end when a suspect is brought to court. This is the time when a suspect is tried for the crime and either acquitted (found innocent) or convicted (found guilty).

Several judges may sit in on important cases. Here, seven judges are considering evidence in the Massachusetts Supreme Judicial Court in the USA.

What happens in the courtroom

A courtroom trial is essentially a battle between the **prosecution** (lawyers trying to prove the suspect is guilty) and the **defence** (other lawyers trying to prove the suspect is innocent). A collection of members of the public, called the **jury**, decide whether the suspect is guilty or innocent after hearing cases (arguments) made by the prosecution and defence.

The jury will see evidence and hear witnesses (including the suspect) being questioned both by the prosecution and the defence. If a witness gives evidence to help the prosecution, he or she is also questioned by the defence, and vice versa. This is called cross-examination and it gives each side a chance to find faults in the other's evidence.

HISTORY FILE

O.J.'S GLOVES
Sometimes powerful evidence backfires when it is presented in court. When former US football star O.J. Simpson was tried for the murder of his wife and her friend in 1995, one of the most important pieces of evidence was a pair of bloodstained gloves found at the crime scene. The prosecution argued that the gloves belonged to Simpson. In an courtroom scene that was televised around the world, Simpson tried on the gloves and found that they were too

A police officer shows evidence during a trial. Evidence is always sealed and labelled to prevent tampering.

Although the jury decides whether the suspect is innocent or guilty, they must follow very clear instructions given by the judge, who is an expert both in the law and in the justice system.

Evidence in court

Not all the evidence collected during a criminal investigation may be used in court. Evidence must be relevant to the case and witnesses must be reliable. There must also be an 'unbroken chain of evidence', which means there must be no possibility that items collected at the scene could have been tampered with in any way. Evidence that doesn't fit these rules is said to be 'inadmissible' and cannot be used in court.

Forensic scientists often appear in court as what are called 'expert witnesses'. They may present facts about their observations or give their expert opinions on things that have been found at the crime scene. Just as the prosecution may use expert witnesses to prove a suspect is guilty, so the defence may use its own experts to prove that a suspect is innocent. Whichever side they act for, expert witnesses are usually cross-examined.

If there is enough evidence, the jury may find the suspect guilty of the crime and the judge will pass sentence (decide on the punishment) according to the crime committed. But even this may not be the end of a criminal investigation. New evidence is sometimes discovered after a trial ends, and new forensic techniques are always being developed. 'Criminals' are sometimes released following a new trial – called an appeal – because new evidence has proved that they were innocent all along.

small for his hands. Despite other evidence linking him to the crime scene, he was found not guilty of the murders. But another trial in 1997 found him liable for the deaths.

The trial of O.J. Simpson made headline news around the world.

GLOSSARY AND FURTHER INFO

Anthropometry A way of identifying people by measuring different parts of the body.

Autopsy The examination of a body to find the cause of death. Also known as a post-mortem.

Behavioural profiling A technique used by criminal psychologists to describe what a suspect is like.

Chain of evidence The idea that evidence must be protected from tampering from the time it is collected at the scene to the time when it is presented in court.

Defence The team of laywers who try to prove in court that a suspect is innocent.

Electrophoresis A technique used in DNA fingerprinting that separates different-sized DNA molecules using an electric current.

Evidence Something that proves a crime has been committed or who committed it.

Forensics The use of science and medicine to solve crimes.

Gunshot residue (GSR) The powder trace left behind on a person's body when they fire a gun.

Identikit A method of reconstructing the face of a criminal from a witness's description.

Jury A group of ordinary people who decide whether a suspect is guilty or innocent in court.

Modus operandi A standard pattern of behaviour followed by a criminal.

Pathologist The forensic doctor who carries out an autopsy or post-mortem.

Physical match An exact match between evidence found in two different places.

Polygraph A lie-detecting machine.

Post-mortem The examination of a body to find the cause of death. Also known as an autopsy.

Prosecution The team of lawyers who try to prove in court that a suspect is guilty.

Reconstruction A re-staging of a crime to jog the memories of witnesses.

Serial killer Someone who kills one person after another, often to a particular pattern.

Spectrometer A piece of scientific equipment used to identify unknown chemicals.

Statement The evidence given by a suspect or a witness to the police.

Suspects People who may have committed a crime.

Toxicologist A forensic scientist who studies poisons.

PLACES TO VISIT

Visit your local police station and ask if you can make an appointment for someone to show you around. Ask if a police officer will take your fingerprints.

West Midlands Police Museum, Sparkhill Police Station, Sparkhill, Birmingham B11 4EA, UK.
Tel. 0121 626 7181.
A police museum based near the centre of Birmingham (open by appointment only).

Fire and Police Museum, West Bar, Sheffield S3 8PT, UK. Tel. 0114 249 1999.
The largest volunteer-run museum of its kind in the UK.

Science Museum, Exhibition Road, South Kensington, London SW7 2DD, UK. Tel 0207 942 4000.
Exhibitions and working models explaining science.

BOOKS TO READ

Crime Lab 101 by Robert Garner (Walker Books, 1992)
Police Lab: Using Science to Solve Crimes by Robert Sheely (Silver Moon Press, 1993)
Talking Bones: The Science of Forensic Anthropology by Peggy Thomas (Facts on File, 1995)
The FBI: Inside the World's Most Powerful Law Enforcement Agency by Ronald Kessler (Pocket Books, 1994)
The Official Encyclopedia of Scotland Yard by Martin Fido and Keith Skinner (Virgin Books, 1999)
The Usborne Detective's Handbook (Usborne, 1989)

WEB SITES

FBI Kids & Youth Educational Page
http://www.fbi.gov/kids/kids.htm

Metropolitan Police Service Homepage
http://www.met.police.uk/

Evidence: The True Witness – Forensic Science
http://library.thinkquest.org/17049/gather/

Wildlife Crime Busters: National Geographic magazine
http://www.nationalgeographic.com/world/9902/crime-busters/index.html

INDEX

Comparing fingerprints

In the original fingerprint system devised by Sir
Edward Henry, two prints were said to match when
16 specific features of one print matched the same
features in the other. Detectives in the United
States believe it is enough to match only 8 or 12
features, but British detectives still insist on 16
matching features.